CONSUMER BEHAVIOUR

SITUN KRUSHNA SAHU

Copyright © Situn Krushna Sahu
All Rights Reserved.

ISBN 978-1-68487-673-0

This book has been published with all efforts taken to make the material error-free after the consent of the author. However, the author and the publisher do not assume and hereby disclaim any liability to any party for any loss, damage, or disruption caused by errors or omissions, whether such errors or omissions result from negligence, accident, or any other cause.

While every effort has been made to avoid any mistake or omission, this publication is being sold on the condition and understanding that neither the author nor the publishers or printers would be liable in any manner to any person by reason of any mistake or omission in this publication or for any action taken or omitted to be taken or advice rendered or accepted on the basis of this work. For any defect in printing or binding the publishers will be liable only to replace the defective copy by another copy of this work then available.

This book is dedicated to my parents

my wife Nibedita, son, Tanmay

and to the employees of KIT

Contents

Preface ix

Acknowledgements xi

About The Author xiii

   1. Consumer Behaviour   1

   2. Segmentation, Targeting And Positioning   5

   3. Motivation   11

   4. Personality   13

   5. Perception   20

   6. Learning   27

   7. Attitude   37

   8. Diffusion Of Innovation   42

   9. Culture   44

  10. Social Class   47

  11. Group Influence   48

  12. Household Decision Making   50

  13. Consumer Decision Making   52

  14. Case Studies   54

"Being truly customer-centric means having a deep understanding of your customers unmet needs"

– Maria Martinez

Preface

Consumer behavior is an imperative subject for study as marketers observe what influence consumers buying decision making process. By this understanding marketer keep those products identified as needed and takeout products that are to be taken out. As such studying consumer behavior augment marketers for presenting the products effectively that generates maximum impact on consumer buying.

Analyzing consumer behavior will be more relevant as it will reveal what consumers think, how they feel about brands, products, what influences product choices, what is their behavior while shopping, how consumers environment family, friends, media has effect on their behavior.

Now a day's consumer in India has aspirations which is variety seeking as they want numerous products and services that exceeds their income. Earlier low price means low quality but, in these days, we have every day low price in retail shops which is meant for consumers to purchase product of high value. Indian consumers are educated and large chunk of these consumers are youth. This changing the way people are shopping. Implication of this has on various aspects of shopping such as the choice of brands. There are variety of Indian and Multi National Company brands available for consumers, which is presented with well thought out merchandise mix.

Consumers behavior in emerging cities is quite different from metro and capital cities. As these could be identified and explored as small pockets of big opportunities. They have characteristics like value for money orientation, local cultural affinity and conservative while spending. Critical is their high purchasing aspirations often constrained by product availability. Brands evoke brand loyalty if they are having right price and performance in product categories. Consumer's in India as their counterparts everywhere else in the world pick the products and services which offers best value. So often consumer behaviour is influenced by different factors. Marketers should study consumer product and services purchase patterns and figure out buyer wants and trends. This book would be quite useful for students of MBA/PGDM, consumers and marketers.

Acknowledgements

Inscribing a book of this nature is an incredible journey for me. Usually it took years of research and experience. This book has come up from numerous seminars I have attended and research papers written and books I have read. There are numerous suggestions from various sources I have had privilege of working. I would like to thank all of those staff in the KIT who spent their time and memories with me. I have benefited immensely from interaction with students, colleagues and staffs of various institutes and companies I have worked with. I am thankful to the publishers for being part of making this book.

About The Author

Situn Krushna Sahu is an Assistant Professor, Writer, Manager, Consultant, Researcher and Marketer. He is currently the Assistant Professor in KIT (Berhampur, Odisha) part of department of Business Management. He has studied Engineering in Mechanical at the BNCOE (Pusad, Maharastra) and Post Graduate Diploma in Management at ICFAI Business School (Hyderabad, Telegana) before taking up a corporate job in ICICI Bank and subsequently academics jobs in GIET, Imperial Institutions.

He grew up with passion for marketing combine with his creative ability for making a career in it. With years of experience in marketing he has complied it in a book of Marketing Management which is useful for academicians and students.

He has rendered his involvement in many conferences, workshops and seminars. He has been a regular visiting faculty to so many Institutes and Universities. Browsing, watching TV, reading, singing, travelling, eating different cuisines and gardening are his hobbies.

CHAPTER I

Consumer Behaviour

Studying consumer behaviour is vital, therefore as a result of this marketers will see what influences consumers' shopping choices of product and services. It is very vital to understand how shoppers evaluate, acquire, use or dispose of goods and services. It generally hovers around

1. Different kinds of decision making that consumers indulge in
2. Kind of strategies can a brand use when consumers search for any information
3. Specific differences in Consumer Decision Making between FMCG products and durables
4. Kind of strategies can a brand use when consumers search for any information
5. Kinds of factors influence the selection of retail outlets when a consumer decides to buy a product

Consumer behavior supports marketers in making choice and decide in presenting their products in such a way that factors in maximum influence on consumers purchase decisions.

Consumer behaviour definition is "the decision process is the activity of consumer engaged in evaluating, acquiring, using or disposing of goods and services."

American Marketing Association defined consumer behaviour is the dynamic interaction of affect and cognition, behaviour, and environmental events by which human beings conduct the exchange aspects of their lives.

Hawkins, Best, and Coney defined Consumer behaviour is the study of individuals, groups or organisations and the processes they use to select, secure, use and dispose of products, services, experiences or ideas to satisfy needs and the impacts that these processes have on the consumer and society.

Satish K. Batra and S. H. H. Kazmi defined Consumer behaviour is the mental and emotional processes and the observable behaviour of consumers during searching purchasing and post consumption of a product and service.

Consumer behaviour covers a broad category of consumers based on their diversity in age, sex, culture, taste, preference, educational level and income level. By means of all of the variety of number of goods and services offered, and the consumer choices, one may speculate how marketers actually reach consumers with their marketing messages.

Understanding consumer behaviour helps in recognizing whom to target, how to target, when to reach them, and what message is to be given to them to reach the target audience to buy the product.

Customer Vs Consumer

'Consumer' is a more comprehensive based term, whereas 'customer' denotes a kind of permanency in the user of the product. We always use the word 'customer' if the consumption is spreads over a period of time. For example, a regular shopper at Food Bazaar for the past one year can be referred to as a customer of that shop.

Mostly the words consumer and customer are also used to represent the differences between the purchaser and the final user of the product. From this perspective, the person who purchases the product from the shop is defined as the customer and the person who uses the product is the consumer.

Citing an example, a housewife purchases a fairness cream from a shop for her daughter. The mother in this scenario is only a customer, but the consumer is her daughter.

Another scenario if the housewife had purchased the fairness cream for herself then she is the customer as well as the consumer. In this situation, customer and consumer are one and the same person.

Consumer Behavior – Past and the Present

Consumer of yesterday didn't had choices to choose from. They have to go to different shops to shop their needs and requirements. Consumers had low buying power and were more cost conscious as compared to brand and quality conscious of today. The focus of yesterday was to fulfil the basic need instead of impressing others.

At present India has the youngest population amongst the major countries. There are a large proportion of young people in India in different income categories. Marketers are often faced with a dilemma about the choice of proper market segment. In India they do not have to face this dilemma largely because rapid urbanization, increase in demand, presence of large number of young populations, and many number of opportunities are available.

These challenges have been created by a combination of several and diverse factors like cultural practices, exposure to Westernization, the emergence of technology-savvy teenagers and young adults, a growing population of senior citizens, the culture of price-consciousness as compared with online retailers like Amazon, Flipkart, the demand for luxury brands, growing hospitality and healthcare, rural consumption of product categories and the growth of modern retailing.

Consumerism

Consumerism is that the organized efforts of numerous people, groups, governments and varied associated organizations that helps to guard the buyer from unfair practices and to safeguard their rights. Largely it's a peaceful and democratic movement for protection against their exploitation.

Consumer is viewed as the king in modern marketing. In a market economy, every effort is made to encourage consumer satisfaction in turn the belief of consumer is given the highest priority.

There are instances though where consumers are generally ignored and sometimes, exploited as well. Therefore, consumers come together for being protective their individual interests. Also consumer movement is can be referred as consumerism.

Dimensions of Consumer Behavior

Consumer behaviour is multidimensional in nature, the following disciplines has its influence

- Psychology may be a discipline that deals with the study of mind and behaviour. It helps in understanding people and teams by establishing principles and researching specific cases. It plays a significant role in understanding how the shoppers behave while purchasing.
- Sociology is that is the study of groups. Once people form groups, their actions are totally different from the actions of these people after they are purchase separately.
- Social Psychology is mostly a combination of sociology and Psychology. It explains how a individual operates in a very complex group. Group dynamics play a very important role in making purchasing choices. Opinions of peers, reference teams, their families and opinion leaders

influence individual in their purchase behaviour.

• Cultural anthropology is that the study of citizens in society. It explores the progress of central beliefs, values and customs that consumers inherit from their parents, that influence their purchasing patterns.

Consumer Behaviour in Digital Era

Compared with traditional product management thought, the significance of the digital domain is important to understand that the consumer may not realize benefit of use of digital method as the best. But then usually find it the best alternative to satisfy his needs given the diversity of needs and the infinite ways to digitally satisfy them.

Digitalization is taking over in online shopping, mobile apps, company websites, books and the conventional modes of entertainment in form of Kindle readers, iTunes and video streaming for entertainments (like Netflix) are few examples of the advancements.

These approaches are likely to spread over to every product category in the near future. Taxi and travel services such as Uber and Ola Cabs are taking the very mundane taxi booking service to its next level through their mobile apps with location capabilities, dynamic demand-based pricing, secure credit card linkages.

*****

CHAPTER II

Segmentation, Targeting and Positioning

STP in marketing is usually for Segmentation, Targeting, and Positioning, a three-step model that examines your products or services along with the way it is communicated its benefits to specific customer segments.

The STP model is a wonderful embodiment of the gradual modification in concentration from a product-centric approach to a customer-centric approach, that allows companies to understand who they are trying to successfully reach and how to position themselves for success.

The main principle behind the progression is to segment your audience in a phased manner, target each segmented group according with their preferences and habits, and build positioning modifications in your branding and marketing strategies to accommodate their needs, desires and expectations.

Segmentation

Market segmentation involves grouping your several customers into segments that have common needs, desires, will respond similarly for a prompt marketing action. Each and every segment will respond to a diverse marketing mix strategy, with each and every segment giving alternate growth and profit opportunities.

Some alternative ways you able to segment your market include the following;

Demographics that focuses on the characteristics of the customer. As an example, these are age, gender, income bracket, education, job and culture.

Psychographics that refers to the customer group's lifestyle. As an example, their social class, lifestyle, personality, perception, and attitudes.

Behavioural that is based on customer behaviour. As an example, online shoppers, shopping centre customers, brand preference and prior purchases.

Geographical location like continent, country, state, province, town, city or rural that the customers resides.

VALS

VALS Segmentation Model discusses to the VALS 2 model that segments consumers into eight classes based on their lifestyles, psychological characteristics, and consumption patterns. Therefore, people term it as the VALS popular consumer segmentation model in consumer behaviour. The VALS is the abbreviation of Values, Attitudes, and Lifestyles and also psychographic factors.

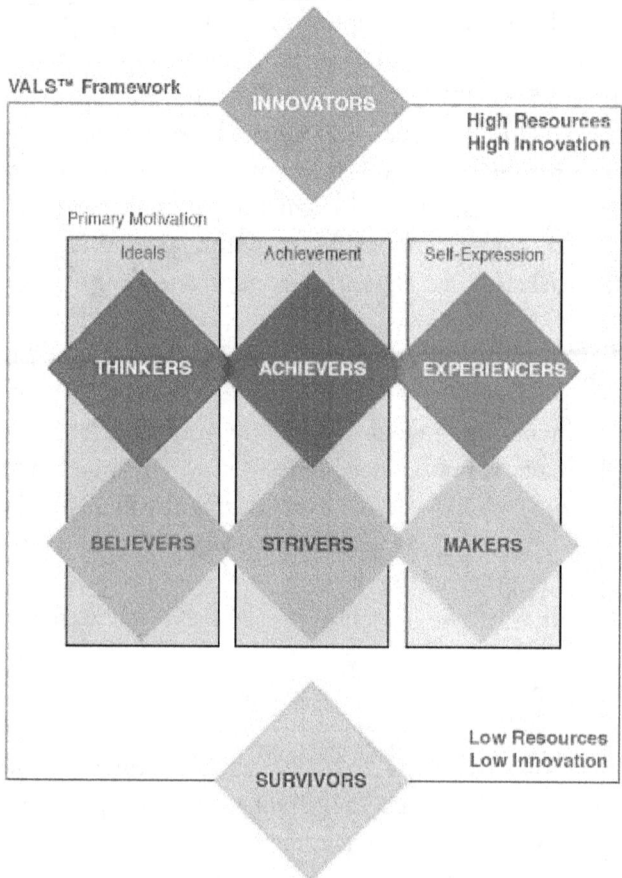

Fig-1

VALS Framework (Fig-1) has 8 Segmentations these are:

1. Survivors
2. Makers
3. Strivers
4. Believers
5. Experiencers
6. Achievers
7. Thinkers
8. Innovators

1. Survivors/ Strugglers

Firstly, Survivors or Strugglers are financially poverty-stricken people.They are poor, low-skilled, ill-educated, deprived of solid social bonds, elderly and passive. They avoid risk owing to feeling powerless. It looks like their prime motive is to meet safety and security demands.

For example, students are survivors.

2. Makers

Makers are practical sensible people with strong traditional values, constructive skills, self-sufficiency, and sufficient income. They live among a conventional context of family, practical work, and additionally also physical recreation. Makers are doubtful of new ideas, politically conservative, and respectful of government authority.

For example, a religious leader having traditional values.

3. Strivers

Strivers are engrossed and interested in others who exhibit qualities that they don't have but that they admire. They inquire concerning about motivation and self-definition. They expect to attain goals through wealth and frequently feel that life has dealt them a bad hand because of the less money. Strivers feel simply bored as a result they are very impulsive.

For example, an unemployed person is looking for a job after completing graduation.

4. Believers

Believers belong to a really conservative and intensely moral mentality similar to makers. They appear like makers owing to having conservative and traditional values. They follow established routines organized by the family, social and religious organizations. Their income, education, and energy are sufficient to fulfil demands.

For example, an mature person retired from government service.

5. Experiencers

Experiencers are actually young, energetic, enthusiastic, impulsive, and rebellious people. They look for a variety of excitements but are politically uncommitted and highly ambivalent concerning about what they believe. They seem like to be connected with outdoor activities, sports, recreational, and social activities.

For example, a teenager is an experiencer.

6. Achievers

Actually, achievers are work-oriented thriving people. They prefer to feel in control of their lives. Additionally, they are also deeply committed to work and keep promises to family, society, and career. Achievers respect authority as a result they like to keeping the promise but are politically conservative.

For example, an employed person is an achiever.

7. Thinkers/ Fulfilled

Thinkers are adequately adult and mature, well-educated, professional people with satisfying financial income. They stay current with international and national events and are usually tend to increase knowledge. They are sometimes calm and confident because they rely on their decisions.

For example, a successful businessman is a thinker.

8. Innovators/ Actualizers

Finally, Innovators are very effective people with self-esteem and substantial resources in contrast to strugglers. Innovators are supervised by each other's principle and by the dreams around them. They want to be a leader in government and business as such they have enormous power and social awareness.

For example, a political leader who can change society with power is an innovator.

Segmentation example

Spice jet focuses on price sensitive consumers who will be allotted seating for low prices and served with meals. In contrary, most airlines follow the differentiated strategy: They offer high priced tickets to those who are uncompromising therein they can't tell beforehand that they have to be compelled to fly in advance when they need to fly and find it impractical to stay over a Saturday. These travellers sometimes business travellers pay high fares but can only fill the planes up partially. The identical airlines then sell few of the remaining seats to more price sensitive customers who can buy two weeks beforehand and stay over.

Targeting

After segmenting the market based on the diverse groups and classes, you got to opt for your targets. No one strategy will ensemble all consumer groups, thus having the ability to develop specific strategies for your target markets is vital.

There are three general strategies for choosing your target markets:

Undifferentiated Targeting: In this approach there is view that the market as one group, so employs a single marketing strategy. This strategy also helpful for a business with little competition wherever you will not got to tailor ways for various preferences.

Concentrated Targeting: This approach focuses on choosing a selected market niche segment on which promoting efforts are targeted. Your firm is that which focus on a single segment thus you will be able to understand the wants and needs of that individual market intimately. Tiny firms usually often benefit from this strategy as focusing on one segment allows them to compete effectively against larger corporations.

Multi-Segment Targeting: This approach is employed if you would like need to target on two or more well defined market segments and want to develop different strategies for them. Multi segment targeting offers several benefits but it can be costly as it involves superior input from management, bigger market research and increased promotional strategies. Prior to choosing a particular selected targeting strategy, you must perform a cost benefit analysis between all available strategical ways and determine which is able to fit your situation best.

Targeting example

While McDonald's features a great reputation for being fast, consistent quality, family friendly food, it might be tough to convince consumers that McDonald's currently offers food of their choice. Thus, McDonald's would in all probability be happier targeting families in search of consistent quality food in nice, clean restaurants.

Positioning

Positioning is developing a product and brand image within the minds of consumers. It also can include refining a customer's perception concerning the experience they are going to have if they prefer to purchase your product or service. The business will definitely influence your business marketing mix, subsequently the perceptions of its chosen customer base through strategic promotional activities.

Effective positioning involves a good understanding of competing products and also the benefits that are sought after by your target market. It additionally needs you to identify a differential advantage with that it will deliver the desired benefits to the market effectively against the competition. Business ought to aim to define themselves within the eyes of their customers with regards to their competition.

Positioning example

Apple Computer being maker of user-friendly computers has chosen to position it like that. Thus, Apple has done a lot through its advertising to promote itself, through its unintimidating icons, as a computer for "non-geeks." The well designed product, in contrast, is aimed a "techies."

*****

CHAPTER III

Motivation

Motivation (Fig-2) is the driving force in individuals made by a state of tension caused by unfulfilled needs and wants. Individuals make optimum effort for reducing this tension by having appropriate behaviour with expectation that it will satisfy their need. Much is depends on consumers thinking and learning in achieving this goals that pattern of behaviour which they believe will satisfy their need. If the consumer's need is fulfilled which in turn reduces the tension in them.

Model of the Motivation Process

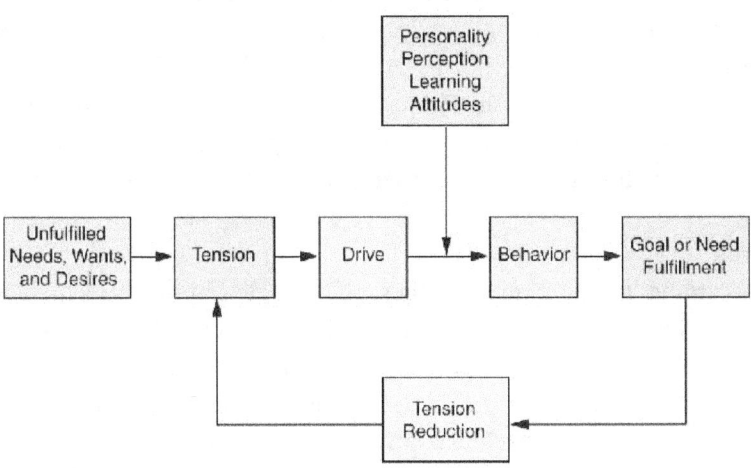

Fig -2

Needs

Everyone has needs. Many needs are basic in nature for sustaining life and they are with the individual when they are born. These basic needs are called as physiological needs or biogenic needs. These include the needs for air, water, food, shelter, sleep, clothing and sex. Physiological needs are essential is denoted as primary needs. While brought up in a culture and society we learn to have acquired needs. These are learnt needs for having self-esteem, prestige, affection, power and achievement. Acquired needs are generally psychological are considered as secondary needs or motives.

Basically, needs classified as utilitarian and hedonic. Utilitarian needs are focused on having benefits and are identified with product attributes which give product performance like economy or durability.

Hedonic needs are associated with achieving pleasure as consumers consume products and services often relate with emotions. Hedonic needs are experiential. Evaluative criteria for brands are generally emotional (Hedonic) rather than rational (Utilitarian).

Goal

Individual needs are goal oriented. Marketers are more interested in consumer's goal-oriented behaviour with product and services. For satisfaction of hunger consumer eat food which is of any type but individual goal may be chicken roast. Goal selection depends on personal experiences, physical capacity, cultural norms and values, if goal object is accessible. Goals are often chosen to satisfy specific needs but also could be perceived as symbolically reflecting individual self-image. We are generally mostly aware of our primary need rather than psychological or secondary needs.

Motives

Classifying motives distinguishes physiological motives, which is for satisfying biological needs of individual like hunger, thirst and safety. Psychogenic motives satisfying psychological needs such as achievement, affection, status and these are learned. Conscious motives people are aware such as hunger but unconscious motives people often are not aware, such as expensive cloths. Positive motives attract consumers but negative motives for avoiding unpleasant consequences

Needs and goals are dynamic keep on recurring, changing and growing as a result of individuals changing physical conditions, environment, experiences, learning and social interactions. If goals are not achieved individuals continue striving for them or may develop substitute goals.

*****

CHAPTER IV

Personality

Definition of personality is according to Gordon W. Allport is "Personality is the dynamic organization within the individual of those psychophysical systems that determine his unique adjustment to environment".

Personality shows the inner psychological characteristics that replicate how a person reacts to his environment. Personality shows the individual choices for various products and brands. It helps with the marketers in deciding when and how to promote the product in the market. Categorization Personality on the basis of individual traits, likes, dislikes etc.

Consumer motivations are forces that stimulates and direct consumers towards performing purposeful goal-oriented behavior and the personality of an individual guides the behavior chosen to achieve specific goals in different situations. Personality of an individual is made up of his inherited characteristics and the interaction with environment and moderated by situational conditions.

Distinct properties of personalities are

1. Personality is used to account for differences between individuals rather than the similarities.
2. Personality is generally believed to be consistent and enduring over time and tends to carry on variety of situations.
3. Despite the fact that personality tends to be consistent and enduring, it may change due to major life events such as marriage, birth, death in a family, change in economic circumstances and the process aging.

Theories of Personality

1. Self-concept theory
2. Psychoanalytic theory
3. Social/Cultural (Neo-Freudian) theory
4. Trait theory

1. Self-concept theory

Self-concept theory focuses on how the self-image of individual consumers influences the purchase behavior. Each of us have self-concept. A popular model proposed by M. Joseph Sergy, there are four specific types of self-images.

Actual self represents what consumers buy or own is a reflection of what they think and believe who they are. What they would like to be is their ideal self, how they feel others to see them is their social self and how they would like others to see them is their ideal social self, how consumers expect to see themselves sometime in future is expected self.

Self-concept theory was related with ego and super ego, which are the two vital concepts of psychoanalytic theory. The ego is believed to be a reflection of individuals objective reality and is similar to the actual self of self-concept theory. The super ego is concerned with the way things should be. Thus, it is a reflection of ideal self. To determine consumer's self-concept, they are asked to describe how they actually view themselves (actual self), or how they would prefer to see themselves (ideal self) on various attributes such as modern, practical, caring, energetic, self-controlled, dependable, aggressive, successful, serious, sensitive, happy, carefree, reckless.

Actual Self

In fact, no one is having actual self because consumers have different role identities. A consumer could be any of these husband, father, employee and a member of some club or voluntary association. In specific situations, one of these roles will be dominant and influence the individual's behavior. The actual self is the result of the combination of individuals with different roles. In accordance with the images they have of themselves consumers actual self-influences their product purchases and thereby attaining self-consistency. An individual has a self-concept, which formed through interaction with parents, peers, teachers, and influential others.

Ideal Self

The concept of ideal self is usually closely related to an individual's self-esteem. The gap between actual self and ideal self-determines the degree of individual's self-esteem. Greater the difference between two, lower the self-esteem. Advertisement themes and images often produce greater discrepancy between consumers actual self and ideal self. Glamour advertising that depicts attractive models and luxurious lifestyles creates a world that is unreachable for most consumers. As a consequence, consumers feel a sense of inadequacy based on a comparison of their actual self with the portrayed idealized images. Advertising tends to pull down consumers self-esteem when it attempts at increasing the disparity between actual self and ideal self.

Extended Self

The concept of extended self recognizes the interaction between individual and the symbols in their environment, thereby meaning that consumers acquire products for their symbolic value in enhancing their self-concept. This also means that consumers buy groups of products that complement each other because of their symbolic association.

While the Rolex watch, Brookes Brothers suit, New Balance running shoes, Sony Walkman and BMW automobiles, on the surface bear no relation with each other, many consumers would easily group these disparate products together as a symbolic whole.

2. Psychoanalytic theory

Freud's psychoanalytic theory proposes that each individual's personality is the result of childhood conflicts. These conflicts are derived from three elementary fundamental parts of personality: Id, Ego, and Superego.

The Id is the source of an individual's strong basic drives and urges such as hunger, sex, aggression and self-preservation. The Id operates on what is called the 'pleasure principle' that is for seeking immediate pleasure and avoid pain. The Id is entirely unconscious and not fully capable of dealing with objective reality.

The ego is the individual's conscious control. Ego operates on 'reality principle'. It is capable of postponing the gratification until that time when it will be suitably and effectively directed towards attaining the goals of the id in a socially acceptable manner. For example, instead of than manifesting aggression in a very anti-social manner, a consumer can partially satisfy this need by buying a powerful motorcycle. The ego is individuals' self-concept.

The super ego establishes the moral part of an individual's personality. It represents the perfect ideal instead of the real, defines what is right and sensibly good and it influences the individual to attempt and strive for perfection. It operates in the unconscious and often represses certain behavior that would otherwise occur based on Id, which could disrupt the social system.

3. Social/Cultural (Neo-Freudian) theory

Carl Jung and Alfred Adler, believed that social and cultural variables, rather than biological drives are more important in the development of an individual's personality. These social theorists, also referred as Neo-Freudian school, viewed individuals as striving to win over feelings of inferiority and searching for ways to gain love, security and relationship. They emphasized that childhood experiences in regarding relating to others in turn produce feelings of inferiority, insecurity and lack of love and affection. Such feelings encourage motivate people to make themselves perfect and they device ways methods to cope with anxieties resulting from feelings of inferiority.

4. Trait Theory

The trait theory states that human personality is composed of a set of traits that describe general response patterns' P Guilford describes a trait as any distinguishing and relatively enduring way in which one individual differs from another. The concept is that traits are general and relatively stable characteristics of personality that influence behavioral tendencies.

Self-Concept and Self Esteem while purchasing a Brand

Smith and Mackie defined it by saying 'The self-concept is what we think about the self; self-esteem is the positive or negative evaluations of the self, as in how we feel about it.'

Some brands make an attempt to connect with the self-concept of consumers. Rin detergent launched a campaign wherein a young girl with her mother makes a 'bold statement' about herself in spite of the negative comments that the hotel manager makes about the girl based on his perception of her 'shabby' clothes. In a subsequent campaign 'Rin' created an impressive portrayal of a young girl in a rural area where an industrialist keeps wondering about qualified personnel in the area (the brand's role in the confidence reflected by the protagonist comes through clearly in both the ads). The Rin Career Academy advertises (along with one of the ads) that it can assist young women to gain skills that will propel them towards professional success. The self-brand connect made possible by the concept of self-esteem is likely to create a strong and favourable associations of the brand in the consumer's mind.

Motivation and personality are powerful concepts as they are closely linked to the self-concept of consumers. Needs, motivation and personality appropriate to consider them together as they are related concepts.Need is a state of deprivation that produces discomfort (widely quoted in literature). Motivation is the drive which impels a person to achieve his/her goals. Personality is a set of inner characteristics that enables a person to decide how he/she should consistently respond to the environment. Motivation and personality are linked— a person with a high degree of confidence may be assertive. There are a number of theories on personality.

The Freudian theory assumes that the behaviour of individuals is based on unconscious needs and drives. Therefore, human personality comprises of three parts— 'id', ego and super ego. 'Id' is the components that are consists of impulses and primitive instincts that urge an individual to seek immediate gratification. The thoughts associated with 'id' are primitive in nature and are associated with baser instincts. A number of product categories, which may not have well-defined functional attributes and are oriented towards sensual pleasure, formulate communication which may appeal to 'id'. Product categories such as Perfume, cigarette, liquor and condom, which are oriented towards the usage of appeals with baser instincts. Axe and Set Wet brands seem to have adopted the 'id' route. The categories mentioned have an association with 'id' in several parts of the world where these are advertised. Liquor brands may resort to surrogate advertising (involves advertising the brand by creating another category) and use 'id'-oriented appeals to the extent permitted by a society. McDowell soda is an example.

There are usually two varieties of needs, primary and secondary. The physiological needs like thirst, hunger and sex are the primary ones. The secondary needs are acquired, such as a sense of belongingness, status and self-esteem. It is in this situation where consumers may not consciously know their secondary needs and that the symbolism associated with brands may appeal to consumers. Some examples that reflect a consumer's symbolism in terms of association with prestige Louis Philippe and Park Avenue in apparel, Mercedes in automobiles and Fastrack in watches. Consumers, are able to gratify their psychological needs by associating themselves with these symbolic brands.

Liril soap was launched in the 70's and the Liril advertisement captured exactly the experience of indulging in a bath. The water-fall, the model indulging in fresh water and the greenery around was in combined effect with the lime soap (offering freshness and a refreshing experience, the green packaging of the brand and the image of lime on the advertisement in TV commercial). The example reflects how psychographics and brand proposition can be creatively combined for the brand success. After such a brand positioning Liril was very successful for a numerous years, (the focus is on the concept rather than on the performance of the brand). The same theme that reflected 'freshness is back' in 2015, was after almost forty years, Liril brought it back.

Brand Personality

For a number of years, in the category of soaps, Hamam, Cinthol and Liril are in the market. Hamam has limited variants. Liril tried a few but Cinthol has had the maximum number of variants. Liril has a very strong Brand personality developed over almost three decades. the The characteristics of Liril is that of 'refreshing', 'enjoyable', 'indulgent' and 'fragrant'. Hamam has been a family soap and it was positioned (at some point in time) as an 'honest and clean' soap without harmful chemicals. Lux, for instance many decades has been using celebrities and is linked with skin-friendliness and glamour. Aramusk was a macho soap launched for men during the 80's. The brand had immense potential to strengthen its personality, being the pioneer in creating a macho soap. Evolving and developing a personality in this category is extremely important for a long-term association with the brand. Lifebuoy with its 'germ-killing' personality is an example.

In the category of scooters, brand LML Vespa created a personality around itself as such when the scooters category was dominated by Bajaj. LML Vespa's projected personality as 'suave, sophisticated is standing apart from the crowd'. Yamaha was strongly identified with 'youthfulness and adventure' during the late 80's. In the recent times, the brand attempted an association with a celebrity popular among the youth. with its path-breaking 100 cc economy valed bike and Hero Honda went on to create Splendor and Passion which redefined the market.The latter was advertised as a classy, lifestyle product. Rajdoot was another bike brand with a very strong 'personality orientation'. Perception it was having as a 'rugged and tough' bike and was even endorsed by a film celebrity who had a similar image. The brand was popular in the rural markets and even in today's context such a brand can be revived through the creative use of imagery linking the contemporary aspects with the personality associations of the past.

Caliber, the four-stroke bike from Bajaj, developed its personality differentiator from other 'macho' associations that were popular with motorcycle brands. Through perseverance, fortitude and spirited approach under adverse circumstances, the imagery descriptions and the storyline of the TV commercial reinforced the idea of self-esteem. While it is true that the functional aspects of a durable brand in any category need to be competitive, with the emotional associations. Through brand personality add to the appeal of the brand (as in the case of LML Vespa or Caliber). Zodiac, the readymade brand of apparel, was probably the earliest of brands to create a personality in this segment with its iconic model symbolizing formal, elegant and professional look.

Allen Solly, with its semi-formal approach of Friday dressing may have appealed to 'non-conforming and casual' executives in software companies and advertising agencies. Raymond, after hammering down its USP of being a 'guide to a well-dressed male' during the 80's, created 'the complete man' during the 90's. During the 80's In the women's wear product category, there were two brands—Vimal and Garden—which successfully attempted a different brand personality orientation. Vimal was showed as 'lively, other-directed and full of verve' and the Garden was oriented towards 'proud, aloof and distinctively classy' self-image. Siyaram suitings has attempted the ethnic route to create a personality association—'young, modern and highly educated with a strong orientation towards the country'. A certain degree of ethnocentrism was also involved and displayed in this approach.

For a niche up-market segment Double Bull and Charagh Din, the readymade brands marketed in Mumbai held significant appeal for consumers. Perception of consumers was that the brands to be 'elegant and exclusive'. Though both the brands advertised in a few up-market media vehicles, the limited availability of the brands also added to the 'exclusive' image. As a number of personality dimensions have been explored and used in the fabric/readymade category, it would be a challenge for new brands entering the category to cultivate a distinctive personality.

*****

CHAPTER V

Perception

Schiffman and Kanuk state that perception is defined as the process by which an individual select, organizes and interprets stimuli into a meaningful and coherent picture of the world.

Perception is that the is straightforward simple method by which individual select, organize, and interpret sensations, that is the immediate response of sensory receptors (such as the eyes, ears, nose, mouth, and skin) because of basic stimuli such as light, colour, odour, texture, and sound. Whatever that activates a receptor is called a stimulus. The study of perception focuses on what we tend to add to raw sensations in order to give them meaning. Every individual interprets the meaning of a stimulus to be consistent with his or her own distinctive unique biases, needs, and experiences.

The three stages of exposure, attention, and interpretation structure of the method of perception. Perception is simply just the method of (i) selecting, (ii) organizing, and (iii) interpreting information data inputs in order to produce meaning so that would support in consumption decision-making. Information processing involves a series of activities by which are recognised, perceived, transformed into meaningful information and stored in memory.

At the exposure phase part, information inputs received are sensations of our sense organs (i.e., sight, taste, hearing, smell, and touch). For example, when we see or hear an advertisement, smell or touch a product, we receive information inputs. These processes are collectively referred to as the process of perception.

Simply put, perception is "how we see the world around us". Totally when different individuals also may be exposed to the similar same stimuli under the same conditions but however each and every individual recognises the stimuli, selects them, organises them and interprets them is unique. Here this is case of each person and it depends on his needs, wants, values, beliefs, personal experiences, moods and expectations. Perception is also influenced by characteristics of the stimuli, such as size, colour and intensity and the context in which it is seen or heard.

Sensation is the immediate and direct response of sense organs (eyes, ears, nose, mouth and skin) to simple stimuli such as an advertisement, a brand name, or a package. Two people can see or hear the same event; however, their interpretation is often completely different. The meaning we allocate to a stimulus depends on the schema (i.e., set of beliefs), which we assign it. Recognizing and evoking the correct schema is vital to many marketing decisions because this schema determines what criteria consumers will accustom to evaluate the product, package, or message.

Perceptual Organisation

We relate incoming sensations to others already in memory, supported on some structured fundamental organizational principles. These principles originate from Gestalt psychology, a school of thought that maintains that people interpret meaning from the totality of a set of stimuli rather than from any individual stimulus. In other words, the concept proposes that "the whole is greater than the sum of its parts."

Use of the Gestalt Process in Advertising

Ads serve the purpose encouraging customers to shop for the advertised product or service. The Gestalt principle, based mostly of simplicity, states that the entire whole is greater than the sum of its parts.

Marketers recognize that individuals recall what they see in a way far higher percentages than what they hear or read. Whether it is a print ad or televised business commercial, viewers should identify and respond to that whole, bring it to the mind, remember it and desire for having it. Its no secret that advertising happening all around us. We might take note of how many ads we are exposed to on your way to work, or in a whole day?

In fact, the average common person is exposed to around 1,200 ads daily. For this reason, marketers have created new marketing promotional techniques to ensure that their ad reaches the buyer, and influences their behaviour in getting purchasing the product.

Many businesses even incorporated from Gestalt concepts into their websites and stores to confirm verify and guarantee ensure user friendliness and expand customer experience.

Figure and Ground

The figure-ground principlestates that one part of a stimulus can dominate (the figure), and different parts recede into the background (the ground). If the figure is dominant, and the eye goes straight to it.

Fig-3

In this Coke ad (Fig-3), the bottles are strategically placed near to one another in the form of a smile. We tend not to realise but automatically group and process these bottles together. So, the consumer associates Coke with smiling, that stimulates feelings of happiness and joy and ends up in a larger inducement for buying the product.

Similarity Principle

The principle of similarity tells us that consumers tend to cluster group together along with objects that share similar physical characteristics. When conducting an ad campaign, marketers have habits of using the gestalt process when reducing the product or merchandise to a basic design style theme, logo or slogan. Consider and think of famous ad lines or instantly-recognizable symbols, like McDonald's golden arches. That symbol image evokes interest that hamburgers and french fries to anyone remotely familiar with advertising, though the logo itself does not show food. Advertisers attempt for individuality when marketing products, therefore the customer doesn't confuse their product with a competitor's item. Yet, under gestalt principles, customers will not confuse fully completely with different products, such as cars and food, or clothes and electronics.

Proximity

Gestalt psychology suggests our minds cluster group things along together if they are close each another. This can be called grouping and involves the law of proximity. As an example, if a product is offered with next to a photo of a celebrity, we tend to perceive both as being associated, which influences us to buy the product.

It may be used on a bigger scale. For a moment consider your local supermarket. Have you ever detected certain merchandise are placed next to one another? For instance, example of fresh strawberries, blueberries and raspberries are all placed next to chocolate dipping sauce. Why? We tend to naturally perceive them as a group, that influences our behaviour to purchase.

Similarly, the diary section that has cheese, meats and olives in the refrigerator is in the midst section of snacks, breads, oils and dips on topmost unit of the fridge. Why? We tend to group this stuff of items together we intend to buy.

Closure

The closure principle states that individual tend to perceive an incomplete picture image as complete. For example, when we hear that only part of a jingle or theme. Marketing strategies ways that use the method of closure principle encourage audience participation, that may increase the possibility so that people can attend to the message. The concept of closure is another form of idea Gestalt concept employed by marketers, and refers to the method way we perceptually complete objects that are in reality not been completed. Usage of this technique in the brand logo or advertisement is successful because it forces consumers to pay additional attention to brand logo or image, which increases the possibility of storing this information in long-term memory and brand recall in the future. Consider the following examples. This is a ketchup ad by Heinz. Did you look twice at this bottle? Initially we intend to see a tomato sauce bottle, however when we look closer to it then it is becomes clear that the bottle is made up of tomato slices, communicating with the buyer of this product its uses fresh, real tomatoes. Yet again this demonstrates how closure increases our attention to ads.

Dynamics of Perception

Perception consists of several elements and involves selection, organization and interpretation of stimuli. All these elements offer useful points to marketers regarding the formulation of communication strategies. Selection of stimulus, as stated earlier, depends on attention that can be brought into communication through contrast.

Jenson & Nicholson, the paint brand, used full-page magazine advertisements with only a few lines of copy to stand out from the rest.Levi's used black and white advertisements in a magazine published with full of colour advertisements to highlight the contrast.Contrast helps a brand to obtain the involuntary attention of consumers.

Brand Positioning and Perception

As stated earlier, positioning has its foundation in concepts of perception. A positioning (or a perceptual map) provides an idea about how consumers perceive brands specific to relevant dimensions. Two dimensions are chosen. They are traditional to trendy and economy to premium. It is possible to map the existing brands and this enables a new brand to enter the consumer's mind. Perceptual maps enable the marketer to provide the competitive angle to the brand.

It should be noted that considerable primary information is required to obtain the two dimensions in a map. When there are more dimensions preferred by consumers in a product category, the marketers need to use sophisticated marketing research techniques to simplify alter the dimensions chosen for the positioning exercise. Positioning that starts as an attempt by the brand to understand the likings of the target segment should be nurtured in the long run to build a sustainable association. Pepsi's association with the younger generation, Titan's depiction of lifestyles for its consumers and Volvo's association with safety are such examples. When a brand develops an additional association, it has to make ensure that the added association supplements enhances the original association without contradicting it. Raymond's association with the 'complete man' lifestyle proposition strengthens its earlier positioning as the 'guide to a well-dressed male' (which was the positioning of the brand during yesteryears).

Perception and Price

Prices have been used by marketers as an input signal to the perception of quality among consumers. It is not uncommon for consumers to equate high prices with high quality, particularly if backed up by appropriate associations like a premium brand name or an up-market retail outlet. In several product categories like televisions, confectionery and fast foods, consumers compare the brand's prices with those of the one they have in mind. These are internal reference prices. A number of brands of colour televisions used to mark the price tag below Rs 10,000 as consumers may have this as their internal reference price. A popular blade among the masses did not increase its price for a long time as this may have affected the perception of consumers. Soft drink manufacturers like Coke, Pepsi and confectionery brands like Cadbury's and Nestle are concerned with price points, especially at the entry level minimum prices. The re-emergence of 200 ml bottles in soft drinks (some years back in the Indian context) and the Rs 5 price point in chocolates or the 50 paise point in confectionery and candies are examples of value perception in the respective categories. External reference prices are those that consumers compare across outlets for the same brand. A price discount offered by many different retail outlets within the class of consumer durables is a good example. A consumer wanting to buy a model of LG TV may compare the external prices for the same brand and its model across all retail outlets. Similarly, for men's readymade wear, leading brands like Louis Philippe, Arrow or Park Avenue may have factory outlets that offer a discounted price for selected products. These outlets may appeal to a segment, which may likely to have the brand after comparing prices across retail outlets. This segment may also be already prepared to select from a smaller variety (designs) if they get the whole brand of their choice at economical outlets. These consumers compare external prices, probably after compromising on the variety. Transaction utility is another factor that has an impact on price perception. This relates to the satisfaction of a consumer that derives from making a deal within a particular price range. This is closely associated related to the internal reference prices. Transaction utility may be applicable to a cross-section of consumers who may predominantly have their satisfaction tied to the transaction limit they have in mind.

Change of Brand Image

In a competitive context, there may be a need or desire for a brand to alter and change its image depending on the product/market situations. There may be a few brands that have successfully transformed their images. Cadbury's Dairy Milk chocolate (moulded version) was positioned towards children during the eighties. As the chocolate market expanded over the years and as adults were also interested in the product category (due to in the changing lifestyle), Cadbury's transformed the brand image of the moulded variant in such a way that it was repositioned for adults. The target segment shifted from children to adults. The warmth proposition of the previous Positioning (a gift for the children as a reflection of parental warmth) gave way to spontaneous and enjoyable 'celebration' associated with everyday life (cricket field dance commercial was a popular TV commercial for the brand).Another instance is Gems, also from Cadbury's. It was positioned for children in the past but now it has been targeted towards adults as well.

*****

CHAPTER VI

Learning

Behavioural Learning Theories

1. Behavioural learning theories are based on the premise that observable responses to specific external stimuli signal are typically known as called stimulus-response (S-R) theories (Fig-4) signify that learning has taken place.

a) As and when a person retorts in a expected way to a known stimulus, he or she is said to have "learned."

2. Behavioural theories are utmost concerned with the inputs and outcomes of learning.

3. Three theories pertinent to marketing are classical conditioning and instrumental (or operant) conditioning and cognitive learning.

Classical Conditioning

Ivan Pavlov was the first to explain conditioning and to propose it as a general model of how learning happens.

a) For Pavlov, conditioned learning results as when a stimulus paired with another stimulus causes a known response and helps to produce the same response when used alone.

b) He used dogs to establish his theories.

c) Dogs were starving hungry and high motivation to eat.

d) Pavlov made bell sound then instantly applied a meat paste to the dogs' tongues, that caused them to salivate.

e) Adequately a number of repetitions of the bell sound, followed almost quickly by the food, the bell alone has caused the dogs to salivate.

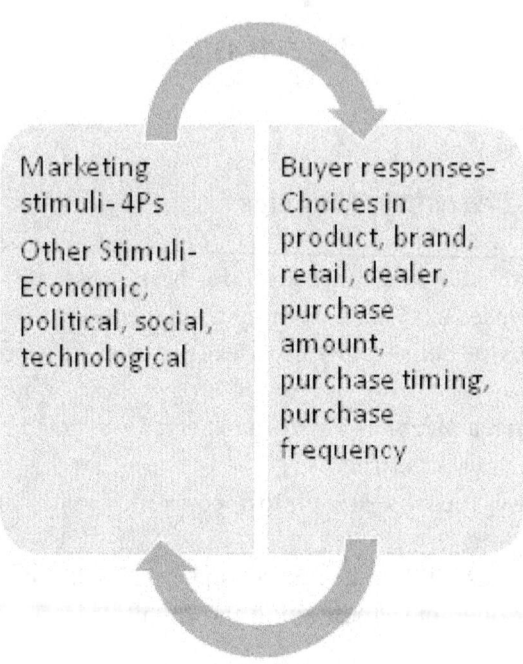

Fig-4

In the context of consumer behaviour, an unconditioned stimulus normally consists of a well-known brand symbol. A former acquired consumer perception of a brand is the unconditioned response. Conditioned stimuli would perhaps contain brand new products under an existing brand name. The conditioned response with belief that would be consumers trying these products so that they embody the same attributes (with which the brand name is associated).

Pavlov (1902) started from the concept that there are some things that a dog does not got to learn. For example, dogs whenever they see food doesn't learn to salivate. This reflex is 'hard-wired' into the dog. In behaviourist terms, it is an unconditioned response (i.e., a stimulus-response association that required no learning).

In behaviourist terms, we write:

Unconditioned Stimulus (Food) > Unconditioned Response (Salivate)

Pavlov showed the existence of the unconditioned response by presenting a dog with a bowl of food and the determining its salivary secretions. In his experiment, Pavlov used a bell as his neutral stimulus. Whenever he gave food to dogs, he also rang a bell simultaneously. After a number of repeats of this procedure, he tried the bell on its own. As you might expect, the bell on its own now caused an increase in salivation.

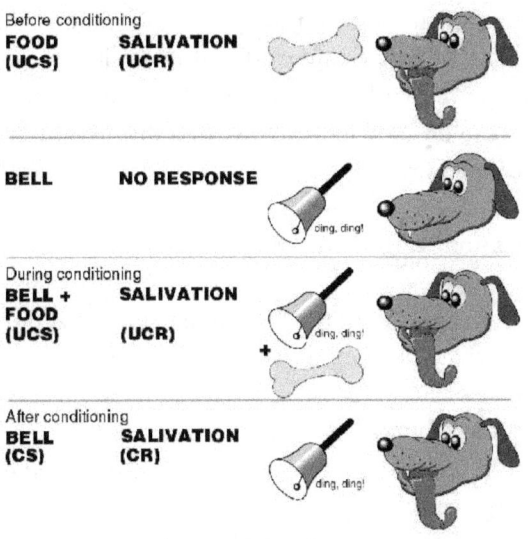

Fig-5

As the dog had educated relate an association between the bell and the food, so therefore a new behaviour (Fig-5) had been learned. As a result of this response it was learned (or conditioned), and called a conditioned response. Now the neutral stimulus has become a conditioned stimulus. Pavlov found that for associations to be created, the two stimuli had to be presented close together simultaneously. He named this as the law of temporal contiguity. If the time between the conditioned stimulus (bell) and unconditioned stimulus (food) is gap is much too great, then learning will not occur.

Since his early work between 1890-1930, Pavlov and his studies of classical conditioning have become famed. Classical conditioning is that it is the first systematic study of basic laws of learning / conditioning and termed it as "classical".

Later developed by John Watson classical conditioning involved learning to associate an unconditioned stimulus that now brings about a particular response (i.e., a reflex) with a new (conditioned) stimulus, so then that the new stimulus brings about the about the same response.

The initial success of Onida based on its 'devil' ad symbolizing neighbour's jealousy used a negative emotion in an interesting manner. In the Indian context Onida was one of the earliest brands in the eighties and probably the first to be advertised on a premium plank. The off-beat execution may have generated interest and taken it into the consideration set of consumers along with a few brands that existed at that time. Fear/negative appeals can be used in a creative and meaningful manner from the viewpoint of a consumer's mind-set.

Strategic Applications of Classical Conditioning

1. Three basic concepts repetition, stimulus generalization, and stimulus discrimination, derived from classical conditioning.

2. Repetition is all of it by increasing the strength of the association between a conditioned stimulus and an unconditioned stimulus and reduces down the process of forgetting.
   a) Attention and retention declines after a certain number of repetitions.
   b) This impact is called as advertising wear out and can be decreased by varied the advertising messages.
   c) By changing the message through cosmetic variation or substantive variation Wear out could be avoided.

3. Some disagree regarding how much proportion of repetition is needed.
   a) The three-hit theory states that the optimum number of exposures to an advertisement is three.
   i) Make the consumer aware of the product.
   ii) Show consumers the relevance of the product.
   iii) Remind them of its benefits.
   iv) Others assume it may take 11 to 12 repetitions to achieve it.

4. The effectiveness of repetition is somewhat dependent upon the number of competitive advertising to which that buyer is exposed.

a) As exposure will increase, the potential for interference increases.

Significant aspect of learning principles is concerned with how consumers learn brand associations. Consumers provide meanings to the offerings made by marketers. Brands evolve their communication strategies that shape brand meanings and consumers perceive these meanings based on their own experience with the brands they use; consumers also form perceptions about the brands pre and post-brand usage. Brands get differentiated from commodities that are sold on price differences. The simple difference reflects the fact that a good brand should not just rely on price reduction eternally, specifically in a dynamic environment. The psychological aspects of branding are illustrated by a popular experiment conducted among consumers. When consumers were asked to choose between unbranded offerings of Pepsi and Coke, they chose Pepsi based on its taste; when the brands were identified and they were asked to choose, so they chose Coke.

Classical conditioning deals with the process of associating messages/feelings/situations with a brand on the assumption that the feelings/messages/situations get strongly identified with the brand. Such a process is aimed at creating the brand's associations in the mind-set of consumers. For example, cricket, films and pranks, besides many other aspects, denote youth associations. Hence, having identified the younger generation as its target segment, Pepsi has used visuals of these three aspects in their brand messages. The basic point in such a context is that there are specific situations, which trigger off pleasant sensations and feelings and these situations are being associated with a brand. When a brand aggressively creates visibility using these visuals for a period of time, consumers may internalize the brand as a part of the feelings and experiences associated with these situations. Pepsi is associated with film stars or cricket celebrities or the fun that young people indulge in.

Associations with brands trigger certain thoughts that are stored in the schema which is a collection of knowledge about a domain that is associated with the consumer. Strong brand associations lead to a brand–consumer relationship.

While there may be arguments about the reality of how a consumer can associate with a brand as a friend, the nature of such associations may not be within the conscious mind-set of the consumer. He/she may find that mentioning the respective category will subconsciously direct them towards the brand.

The following have to be taken into account before a brand decides to use a specific feeling/situation:

1.Researching the market is a prerequisite, as a suitable emotion is required to be paired with the brand. The emotion or a specific situation, (which may be called based on the relevant stimulus) is likely to be the core aspect of the brand imagery and has to be selected with great care. When an international brand of jeans entered the Indian market, the brand chose a celebrity who may not have appealed to the target segment of the brand.

2.The imagery selected to be paired with the brand, should have some relevancy to the product category. Selecting a heart-warming emotion for a brand of photographic film is very meaningful as warmth is closely related to bring back the nostalgia or memories. This becomes the brand's benefit for the consumer.

3.It is essential for a brand to plan a specific emotional proposition (it can even be functional) to ensure that the brand offers a sustainable differentiation in the long run.

Stimulus Generalization

The principle of stimulus generalization is useful for the marketers to product line, form, and category extensions. For an already established brand in product line extensions, the marketer adds related products, knowing that the new product is more likely to be adopted when it is related with a known and trusted brand name.

Family branding is the marketing practice of a whole line of company products under the same brand name as with the alternative strategy that take advantage of on the consumer's ability to generalize favourable brand associations from one product to the next.

Stimulus Discrimination

Stimulus discrimination is the opposite of stimulus generalization. The consumer's ability to discriminate among similar stimuli is the basis of positioning strategy, which seeks to establish a unique image for a brand in the consumer's mind. The key to stimulus discrimination is effective positioning, a major competitive advantage of the company. Product or service success made by having the image or position in the mind of the consumer.

For Example, Bajaj, Philips, Sony, Lakme, Pepsi and Coke follow a policy of stimulus generalisation and use family branding. But on the other hand, HUL, P&G and ITC avoid it and employ stimulus discrimination.

Instrumental Conditioning

According to American psychologist B. F. Skinner, most individual learning occurs in a controlled environment in which individuals are "rewarded" for choosing an appropriate behaviour.

a) Instrumental conditioning (R-S) recommends that consumers learn by means of a trial-and-error process in which some purchase behaviours result in getting the more favourable outcomes (i.e., rewards).

b) A learned individual repeat specific behaviour for a favourable experience.

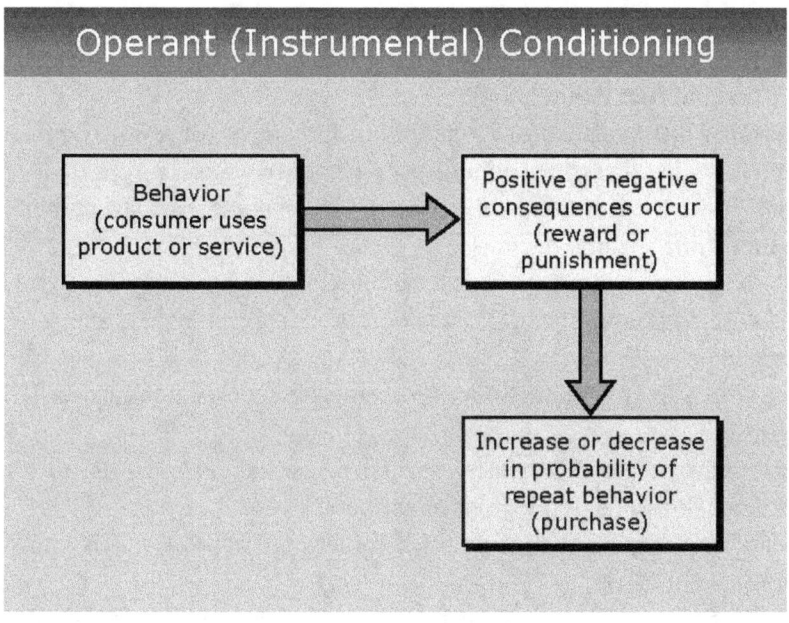

Fig-6

Like Pavlov, Skinner (Fig-6) developed his model of learning by working with animals. For instance let us assume that in a Pavlov like experiment, dogs or rats are provided with two levers instead of one .Pushing one lever will produce food (reward) and in other an electric shock (Punishment).Learning occurs because the consequence of a repeated behaviour is rewarding. In a marketing context, the consumer who tries several brands and styles of jeans before finding a style that fits her figure (positive reinforcement) has engaged in instrumental learning.

Instrumental conditioning is a concept which deals with the desirable reward a consumer gets when he gives a favourable response. A brand of shampoo may prove to be a good choice for dandruff and a brand of readymade wear may be both comfortable and appealing to the peer group of the consumer. Service provided at retail outlets (quick check-out during peak hours in a retail outlet like Food world) can also reinforce consumer behaviour in terms of repeat buying or patronizing a retail outlet. This conditioning can also be applied creatively on the Internet. The basic assumption of applying these principles on the Internet is that reinforcement of this behaviour can also result from the experience (and not only from a good product) provided to consumers.

Reinforcement of Behaviour

Skinner distinguished two types of reinforcement (or reward) influence, which provided that the likelihood for a response would be repeated.

a) Positive reinforcement, consists of events that strengthen the likelihood of a specific response.

b) Negative reinforcement is an unpleasant and negative outcome that also assists to boost a specific behaviour. It is the result of fear appeals in ad messages.

c) Both positive or negative reinforcement can be used to cause a desired response.

d) Extinction and forgetting—when a learned response is no longer reinforced, it results in the point of extinction.

e) With the passage of time often forgetting happens; this is known as the process of decay.

f) Marketers can overcome forgetting through repetition of ads and can combat extinction through the deliberate enhancement of consumer reinforcement.

g) Regularly frequent shopper programs are built on enhancing positive reinforcement and encouraging continued patronage of products and services.

h) Relationship marketing— another form of non-product reinforcement is developing a close personalized relationship with customers.

Gamification makes routine actions into interactive experiences by adding gaming elements. It has some degree of uncertainty, short and long-term goals, feedback, competition that is not hostile and a digital platform. Fitocracy is an app that has gaming principles for physical fitness and awards badges to the user after completing a milestone. Vitality is a game in which players can exchange points for groceries and air tickets. Closer home, apps like Zomato has introduced its own gamification features. Online grocery apps in India too may start such initiatives. Basic principles of instrumental conditioning is used by digital initiatives that have rewards built in them.

A company can plan a contact program with consumers after the sale is over. Instrumental conditioning, in such a situation, triggers off (customer relationship management) CRM. The satisfaction phase immediately follows the purchase phase. The customer wants to fully explore the product using its features, finding out its benefits and experiencing how he/she has benefited from the purchase. Though the 'reward' is the benefit itself, it may be worthwhile for a marketer to reinforce the customer's decision of selecting the brand. This reinforcement may start with a personalized 'thank you' letter and be followed up by company personnel by explaining the brochure accompanying the brand and/or taking a personal interest in familiarizing him/her with the product.

Cognitive Learning

Cognitive learning (S-S) given by Tolman occurs when a person has a goal and must search for and process data in order to make a decision or solve a problem. Wolfgang Kohler's work in the 1920s with apes has furnished important insight into cognitive learning .One of his experiments with a chimpanzee, placed in a cage with a box and a bunch of bananas was hanging from the top of the cage, which was beyond its reach. After several failed attempts to get the bananas, the chimp placed the box under the bananas bunch and jumped from the box top to get it. In this experiment chimpanzee's learning was not based on trial and error. It was a direct outcome of cognitive activity that led to sudden insight into problem solution. In this experiment important is the problem solving approach that was the result of focused thinking. According to cognitive theorist learning is an intellectual activity based on based on complex mental processes involving motivation, perception, formation of brand beliefs, attitude development and change, problem solving and insight. As we acquire more experience and familiarity with different products and services, our cognitive ability and learning increases to compare various product attributes.

*****

CHAPTER VII

Attitude

Consumer attitude may be defined as according to Gordon W. Allport is "Attitude are learned predispositions to respond to an object or class of objects in a consistently favorable or unfavorable way".

Attitude (Fig-7) is composed of cognitive (knowledge), affective (emotional) and conative (behavioral) components. Objects could be specific to consumption or marketing related things (product category, product, brand, service possessions, issues, people, ads, price or retailer).

Attitude towards an object believed to be function of

1. Strength of each belief the individual holds about various attributes of the object
2. Evaluation he/she gives to each belief as it relates to the attitude object

Belief denote the probability an individual attach to a given piece of knowledge as being true. Attitudes are learnt. Attitudes are formed as a result of what we learn from our personal experiences with reality in product usage, exposer to advertising, word of mouth information from relatives, friends and acquaintances.

Attitudes are consistent but not necessarily unchangeable. For example an Indian consumer may have a highly favorable attitude towards German cars but for affordability he/she finds Maruti esteem as more realistic choice.

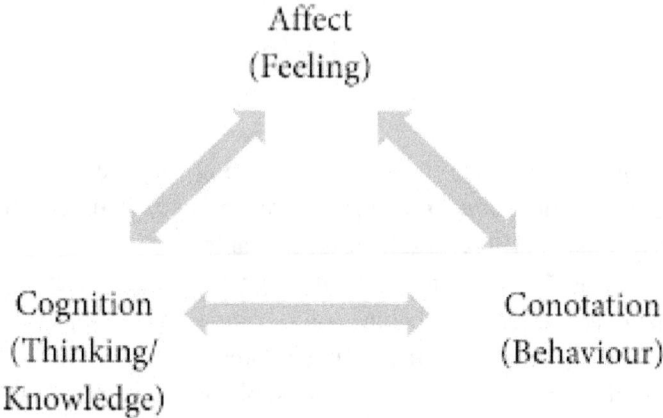

Fig-7

Functions of Attitudes

The following are the functions of attitudes

- **Utilitarian Function-** Attitudes helps people in achieving desired benefits. Certain brand attitudes are partly because of brands utility. If a product has given benefit in the past our attitude towards it will be more favorable. If a consumer considers quick relief as a criterion in selecting anti cold drug he/she will go for a brand that offers it.
- **Ego Defensive Function-** Attitudes are formed protect the ego, self-image, from anxieties and threats. We all are bothered regarding our self-esteem and image so that the product boosting our ego is the target of such a form of attitude. Products advertised in this are mouthwash, toothpastes, deodorants, anti-pimple creams and cosmetics. Advertisement show the fear element, social embarrassment, rejection which discourage consumers and they have negative attitude. Also, social acceptance, confidence, appreciation in ads encourages consumers having positive attitude.
- **Value Expression Function-** Attitudes usually represent the self-image, values, and outlook the individual possess. We gain values, though our upbringing and training. Our positive attitudes towards being in fashion, young man buying motor cycle may be of macho, dominating person who likes purchasing a Royal Enfield Bullet or a Bajaj Pulsar. Our value

system boosts us to buy certain products. For example, our value system disallows us to purchase products such as cigarettes, alcohol, drugs, etc.
- **Knowledge Function**– Individuals' continuously needs knowledge and information. When an individual gets information about a specific product, he creates and modifies his attitude. It store relevant information and ignore what is inappropriate. Advertising is means by which consumers get required information.

Model of Attitude

It denotes how attitudes (Fig-8) are formed and the relationships between attitudes and behavior.

Tri-component Model – According to tri-component model, attitude consists of the following three components.

1. Cognitive Component (Knowledge, Beliefs)
2. Affective Component (Emotions, Feelings)
3. Conative Component (Behavior)

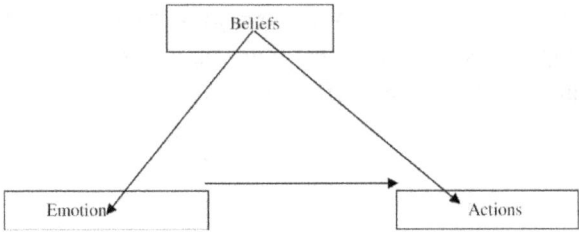

Fig-8

Cognitive Component– Consumers beliefs about products for its attributes. Belief are based on knowledge, experience and perception about attitude object.

A individual may belief that Thumps UP

1. Popular with youngsters
2. Sweet
3. Lot of Caffeine
4. Affordable Price
5. Brand

Affective Component–

Feelings and emotional reactions relate to consumers overall evaluation of the attitude object. Consumer says I like Thumps Up and Thumps Up is not good is a result of affective evaluation. Evaluation could be good or bad. It can be expressed as happiness, elation, sadness, shame or anger.

The second part is the affective component. This consists of a person's feelings, sentiments, and emotions for a particular brand or product. They treat them as the primary criteria for the purpose of evaluation. The state of mind also plays a major role, like the sadness, happiness, anger, or stress, which also affects the attitude of a consumer.

Consumer evaluates products based on specific situations, if situation changes evaluation may change. A student studying for a test believes that drinking Thumps Up keeps him alert believes in the caffeine content it is having. The same student avoids drinking it after test is over.

Conative Component–

It is the likelihood or tendency of an individual to respond in a certain manner towards an attitude object is behavioral conative component. Conative component is treated as intention to buy. Series of decision after a research on it in tendency to buy a Canon Bubble jet printer and recommend it to friends is reflecting behavioral component of attitude.

Attitude can be defined as a mental predisposition favourable or unfavourable, positive or negative towards a person, concept, product, brand, service or an idea. Mental statements which may be concerned with any facet of life, religion, nation, product or brand are Beliefs. But values are an consumer's convictions about his/her mode of living in a very specific cultural setting. Values point out to the individual on how he/she should set and accomplish his/her own goals in life. Shopping for products and service and buying it is one of the major activities of an consumer's life and hence his/her beliefs, attitudes and values are important from the marketer's viewpoint. Values shape attitudes and beliefs and it differs from beliefs.

A belief is what an individual think about the several aspects of his/her life. In the marketing context, an individual may believe (for instance) that a number of product categories marketed by Godrej. Several components held by an attitude, which are an outcome of interrelated beliefs. The attitude of the individual towards Godrej will consist of

i. additional beliefs which are attributes and positive aspects of the company's products and its service,
ii. his/her behavioural response towards Godrej
iii. specific feelings towards Godrej. (Feelings have an emotional component and can get developed because of a variety of reasons)

In this situation, a value that may influence the individual's attitude towards Godrej may be a strong preference towards environment-friendly, green products. With regard to its products and has a strong preference for such products, it is likely to have a positive impact on his/her attitude towards the brand if he/she believes the company is environment-friendly. All beliefs need not necessarily become attitudes, –inter- related beliefs build attitudes. Usually a consumer will have a large number of beliefs, fewer attitudes and even fewer values. Soulflower is a cosmetic brand that is creating an attitude towards vegan-based offerings in India.

*****

CHAPTER VIII

Diffusion of Innovation

Ability for developing successful new product is crucial to company's success (Sale, Future growth and long-term survival). As given by Hubert Gatignon and Thomas S Robertson, an innovation is a product, service, attribute, idea that consumers within a market segment perceive as new and that has an effect on existing consumption patterns. ATM facility was introduced ICICI Bank is new service for consumers in India.

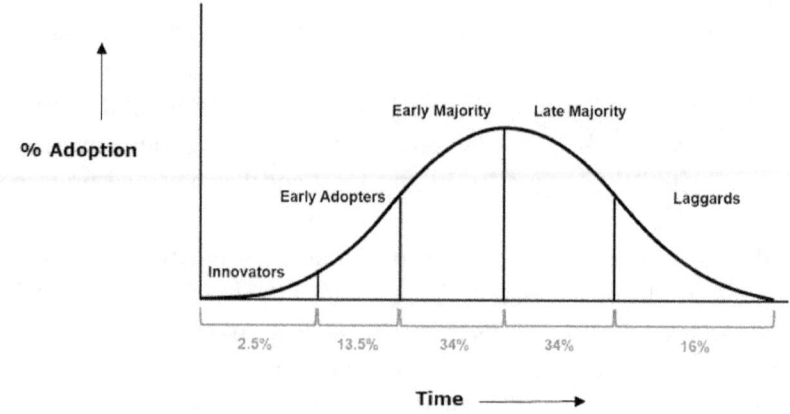

Fig-9

Many products which are new to certain market segments. Like consumers use personal computers in developed countries in eighties, but consumers of developing countries used it in nineties.

Innovation (Fig-9) brings a change in consumers consumption pattern. As internet shopping, which altered the way we shop specific products and services. Microwave ovens have changed the way food is cooked and e-mail have changed the way we communicate. Music players and DVDs store hundred music and video files as compare with seventeen or eighteen songs in CDs.

Types of Innovation

Continuous Innovation

It does product alteration on a continuous basis. Products like newer models of computers and autos.

Dynamically Continuous Innovation

It is requiring changes in the way we acquire, use and dispose products reflect in change in behaviour. As with products like Internet shopping, digital camera, notebook computers, electric cars and cordless phones.

Discontinuous innovation

It is with the products that are new that buyers did not have known it as before. Products such as electric bulbs, aeroplanes, computers, television, photocopying machines, printers, heart transplant, and MRI scanning.

Functional Innovation

It provides functional benefits to consumers over existing alternatives. Like computer laptop offer portability as compared with stationary computers.

Diffusion Process

Across a market innovation spread over time to other consumers is the method of diffusion process. In product life cycle there is Introduction to maturity. Also, in diffusion process there are associated categories of adopters with time of adoption.

Identification of diffusion process begin with innovators in introductory period, early adopters in growth period, early majority and late majority in maturity period and laggards (late adopters) in last for adopting the product.

Innovators – Marketers objective is establishing distribution, building brand awareness in target market and encouraging trial

Early Adopters – broadening product appeals, Growing product availability by increasing its distribution

Early majority and Late majority – brand mature, competition intensify, sales begin steady, price appeals, starts sales promotion, Product modification for getting competitive advantage

Laggards – Lower prices, revitalising the brand, harvesting or divesting.

*****

CHAPTER IX

Culture

Influence of consumer culture with norms and values established by society in which they live. Study of culture is associated with a through examination of factors such as language, religion, knowledge, laws, art, music, work pattern, social customs, festivals and food of a society. Culture includes everything that influence on behaviour is usually taken for granted reflected in its personality and impact of culture is automatic and almost invisible.

D J Mccort and Naresh K. Malhotra have defined culture as the complex whole that includes knowledge, belief, art, law, morals, customs and any other capabilities and habits acquired by humans as members of society.

In a particular framework of culture, individual and household lifestyle evolve. Boundaries set by culture on behaviours are referred to as norms, taken from cultural values, and certain rules permitting and prohibiting certain kind of behaviour. Persons breach cultural norms face sanctions, which can be mild or severe.

Culture are not static but change over time. Marketing can change cultural values and influence it. Advertising agencies, fashion design houses, music companies and cinema are all producers of culture. They create and produce product and services designed meeting cultural goals. It influences desire of consumers to be beautiful, independent and socially recognised. Symbolic goods such as cigarettes, soft drinks, clothing as well as experiential goods such as music, movies and tv programmes impacts the culture and desired lifestyles of consumers of importing nations.

Cultural Values

Cultural Values are enduring beliefs that a given behaviour is desirable. These serve as standards that guide our behaviour across various situations. Values are ingrained in most of us.

Social Value – It represent normal behaviour for a society or group

Personal Values – It define normal behaviour for an individual

Global Values – It denote our core value system. Values are strongly held by us and enduring. Our political philosophy based on freedom, democracy and secularism. We believe in must haves like freedom of speech, for going anywhere we want and dress the way we like.

Shalom H. Schwartz and Wolfgang Bilsky divided global values into seven categories. These are

1. Maturity
2. Security
3. Pro-Social behaviour (doing nice things for other)
4. Restrictive conformity
5. Enjoyment in life
6. Achievement
7. Self-direction

In global categories there are two types of global values. Terminal values are those which are desirable such as freedom, equality, wisdom or comfortable life. Values needed for accomplishing terminal values we have Instrumental values. These include loving, helpfulness and honesty which are required to achieve equality that is a terminal value.

Attitudes and Values

Individuals may possess thousands of attitudes but are likely to have possess less than hundred values. Attitude is learning predisposition if individuals to evaluate and respond to objects, situations or behaviours in a favourable or unfavourable manner. It focuses directly on objects, situations and behaviours. Value go beyond objects and situation and deal with modes of conduct (instrumental values) and highly desirable end states of existence (terminal values). Values are referred as standards how to act, what to want and what attitudes to hold.

Etiquette

It is the general accepted way of behaving in social situations.

In western culture - View unacceptable social behaviour such as noisy eating and belching, eating meal using fingers and not with knife and fork. American males sit cross-legged. Japanese executives rarely say 'no' but say 'that would be difficult'. While talking and looking directly at eyes of another person is considered as aggressive and rude.

In India- We usually eat meal with hand and fingers. Across subculture the voice pitch and gestures generally vary.

Generation X

1. Generation born between 1965 and 1978 in America
2. Higher percentage born in India paid more attention for obtaining a degree
3. Difficult economic conditions
4. Dual income households
5. Job opportunities declining
6. Population pressure
7. Migration for jobs
8. Path to success is difficult
9. Marketers target this group with job promises, autos, appliances, computers and internet

Generation Y

1. Born between 1978 and 1994
2. Equal employment opportunity for woman
3. Dual income households
4. Small family size
5. Owns time saving appliances like computer and Internet.

*****

CHAPTER X

Social Class

In all society, social class can be viewed as a range of social positions in a society.

Social class defines the ranking of people in a society into a hierarchy of distinct status classes generally upper, middle and lower, so that the members of each class have relatively the same status based on their power and prestige.

Social class refers as social standing which is one person's position relative with others in society. Social class based on demographic variables like education, occupation, income, ownership and heritage which we aspire for and hold high esteem. The criteria for social class differs from country to country. In a country education may be accorded as greater prestige while in other politicians or business people may be the choice. Status in a society is determined by following factors like authority, political, economic, military, religious power, ownership of properties, income, occupation, lifestyle, consumption pattern, education, public service, ancestry and connections. Symbols of status such as our possessions as the house we live in, the cars we own, the clothing's we wear or the watches we wear are indicators of social class.

American class structure was proposed by W Lloyad, and has identified six social classes as

1. Upper-Upper
2. Lower-Upper
3. Upper-Middle
4. Lower-Middle
5. Upper-Lower
6. Lower-Lower

Products and services are seen to possess personal and social meanings in addition to their functional characteristics. Members of same social class tend to associate and interact with each other. Social class is fair indicator of consumption patterns in a large number of product categories.

*****

CHAPTER XI

Group Influence

Groups serve as one of the main agents of consumer socialisation and learning and can provide influence for inducing socially acceptable/ unacceptable consumer behaviour.

Group is defined as two or more individuals who share a set of norms, values or beliefs and have certain implicitly or explicitly defined relationships to one another such that their behaviours are interdependent. Reference group is one whose presumed perspectives or values are being used by an individual as the basis of his /her current behaviour. Thus, individual use reference group as guide for behaviour in a specific situation.

Group of Harley-Davidson motorcycle owners, a member of the group depends on other members for information and advice relating to the motorcycle. A new member take suggestion in information about the motorcycle. Group's particular members are considered as knowledgeable and reliable for advice than others. Group leader leads the pack. He gains more respect and authority.

Types of Reference Group

In membership group the member of a reference group could be family. Same individual may desire for belonging to a cricket club said to be aspiration group. A disclaimant group in which individual join and then reject the groups value. In dissociative group an individual may regard membership in the group as undesirable and avoids it. Membership group and aspirational group viewed as positive, marketers advertise to be part of this group. But for disclaimant and dissociative groups are viewed as negative and marketers avoid them.

Nature of reference group

Reference group establish certain norms, roles, status, socialisation and power.

1. Norms: It is generally defined rules and standards of behaviours that the group establishes.

2. Values: These are shared beliefs among group members with what behaviours are appropriate or inappropriate.
3. Roles: It refers to functions that an individual assumes or group assigns to him/her for accomplishing group objectives.
4. Status: it is achieved position that the consumer occupies within the group's hierarchy.
5. Socialisation: it refers to the process with which new members learn the group's system of values, norms and expected behaviour.
6. Power: Influence of a group with members behaviour is closely related with power.

i. Reward Power: It refers to the group's ability to reward a individual
ii. Coercive Power: It relates with power of a group to use disapproval, withholding rewards or punishing the individual
iii. Expert Power: It influences the results from the experience expertise and knowledge of the individual or group.
iv. Referent Power: It flows from the feelings of identification that the individual has with the members of the group.

Products that consumers have informational influence are when products are technologically complex such as computers, laptops, autos, air conditioners and washing machines. Consumers tend for objective evaluation on products selection like insurance policies, or tax saving schemes which are having informational influence.

*****

CHAPTER XII

Household Decision Making

It consists of two or more related individual living in their own or rented accommodation. In recent times in India, it was witnessed a western style nuclear family in urban set up compare with joint family system of past. Nuclear family consist of two married adults of opposite sex with children.

Family is the basic consumption element for several consumer products and services. Consumption of individual members of family is quite same as other households. Buying a bike for a student in a family means sacrificing funds which could have been used for buying micro oven or air conditioner. Role of family in the decision making that is joint decision of its members for items such as tvs, home theatres, computers, vehicles and home appliances.

Willian Wells and George Gubar has given eight stages to make the family Life cycle. These are the following lifecycle stages of family.

1. The bachelor stage: Young, single person under age of 35 years. Income is generally low as they had taken a start to their careers. They have sufficient income and few financial burdens.
2. Newly married: Young couple and no children. Couple are employed and have sufficient income.
3. Full nest I: Young married couple with youngest child is under 6 years of age. There will be greater squeeze in income.
4. Full nest II: Young married couples with children from 6 years to 12 years of age. Better financial position. Children spend mostly time outside home.
5. Full nest III: Older married couples with dependent children living at home. Financial position of the family is good. There is an increase college education cost of children.
6. Empty nest I: Older married couples with children outside home. High income with greater savings.
7. Empty nest II: Older married couples retired with children outside home. Couples live with retirement benefits and drop in income.
8. Solitary survivor: Older single person with low income and medical need and cost.

Basic functions of family include emotional and economic support. Product consumption patterns of individuals are similar with those of other family members. If two or more family members is making a purchase decision then it is known as family decision making. Family roles include influencers, gatekeepers, information gatherers, deciders, buyers and users. Usually a family's approach for decision making influence purchase situations include social class, lifestyle, roles, purchase importance, risk, family life cycle stage.

*****

CHAPTER XIII

Consumer Decision Making

Consumer's buying decisions (Fig-10) and subsequent consumption process of product and services happen with specific situations. It is important for understanding how internal and external influence affect the purchase decision process. By introducing a new product category with a new concept, marketers have to do concept selling at the need stage. This is the stage where the actual and desired state of the consumer is examined. 'Ceasefire', the mini fire-extinguisher kick-started a wave of demand for the product among households (The brand does not retain its hold over the market for a variety of reasons but the objective was to reflect on how the brand used an approach to market was a new concept). It has marketed the concept using the primary advertising. The idea of introducing its mini version of fire extinguisher was a novel idea though the concept of fire-extinguisher, by itself, was not new to the market. So it triggered off a perception of being a very different product than the huge, unwieldy ones encountered in office buildings or movie theatres. The primary advertising (with fear overtones) said different kinds of fires required different kinds of extinguishing gases and Ceasefire was the answer to the need. Concept-selling discusses the product benefits and how these can be solved by taking into consideration the existing problems of consumers and helps them reach a 'desired state'.

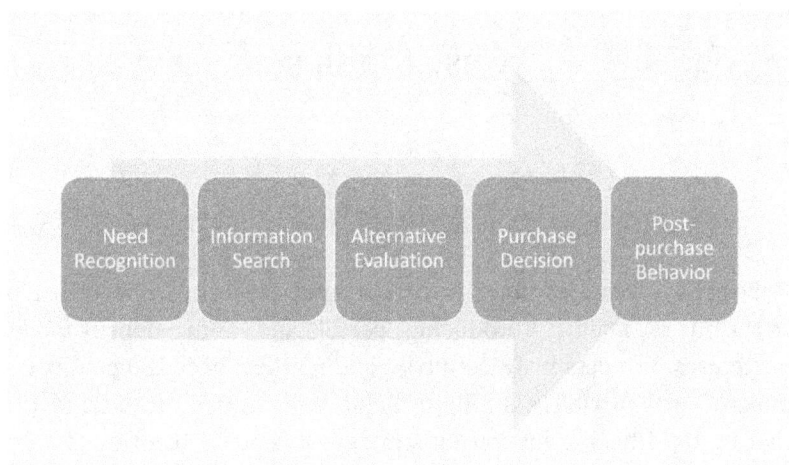

Fig-10

While primary advertising concentrates more on product benefits for the product, the secondary advertising discusses the brand. By way of the secondary advertising it has to supplement the needs of primary advertising for confirmation that the brand gets the competitive advantage of having promoted the concept. A revolutionary brand usually brings in a new-concept product, because of its brand-building efforts. Titan may not be a pioneering brand in quartz watches but it is currently one of the leading watch brands.

*****

CHAPTER XIV

Case Studies

Kellogg's

Kellogg is a branded food manufacturing MNC in India based from America. It is majorly producing cereal and convenience foods. It manufactures products in 18 countries and markets over 180 countries has revenue of around US$14.8 billion. Begin with initially it entered Indian market in 1994 having marketing strategy of foods categories like crispy breakfast.

India's culture of having heavy breakfast which is served hot. As such Kellogg entered Indian market with not much aware of consumers product consumption of cereal with hot milk but creating a motive for use of the product with cold milk. Contradictory to claims made by the company, Indians started to use cereal product with hot milk which made the crispy flakes soggy. As such consumers could not accept as corn flakes as total breakfast and many of them remain hungry. It resisted the usual consumption of ideal hot, spicy and varied regular usual breakfast. Then the company realised about it quite restructured entire marketing strategy to introduce the product as All Day Meal from Crispy breakfast food. Subsequently emphasized nutritional values while branding in India. Increased market share of breakfast cereals in India because of urbanization and increased income of Indian middle class. The breakfast cereal market in India is composed of hot cereals (bran, oats, and wheat bran) and ready-to-eat (RTE) cold cereals (wheat flakes, cornflakes, and muesli). Compared with Ready to-eat (RTE) cold cereals western countries Indians usually prefer hot breakfasts. So this segment is increasing at a more rapid pace. As consumers are nowadays became more health conscious cornflakes dominate market but find competition with product varieties such as oats and muesli which are growing more rapidly than cornflakes. Kellogg's now is worried about it made marketing strategic changes and in turn anticipated there will be a surge in demand of breakfast cereals.

So it made the following

v. Convenient meal
v. Easy to prepare food
v. Complete your diet
v. Foods with higher nutritional and lower calorific values
v. Keep you fit and healthy with products like Chocos, Honey Loops

With iron-Shakti Plus and Special K Kellogg's Cornflakes is started targeting various segments of the society. Pricing in marketing strategy like launching small size convenient packets of Rs10, for price sensitive consumers. It also launched as campaign with catchy punchlines with USP like 'jago jaise bhi,lo Kelloggs hi', 'Andar se khush, to bahar se khush', 'Shuruvat sahi to din sahi' which encouraged the consumers motives and energy levels. Further also company did celebrity endorsements taken stars of television industry and bollywood as on the basis of fitness. Brand Kellogg's Special K projecting Lara Dutta as its brand ambassador in its ads. Not only Kellogg's was the one, Nestle another multinational firm too has successfully ventured in India with its product 'Maggie' and it succeeded because it got one thing right, that is, the hot part of Indian food habits.

Today Indian market alone contributes 10% to the parent's Asia-Pacific revenues of the company. Kellogg India is becoming fastest growing market in the region. Company is now planning for investing triple its size in Indian market and has optimism of taking growth as 20% in coming next five years. Innovations which is India centric and also customization of products, revamping the positioning strategy and single-serve rationally priced packs are some of the key motives behind the success of Kellogg's marketing strategy in India.

• • •

McDonald's

McDonald's is the largest food service retail corporation best known for hot and fresh fries, Hamburger, chicken products, breakfast items, warps desserts. It is serving around 68 million customers daily in 199 countries across more than 36,000 outlets. It was founded in United States of America in 1940. Slogan of McDonald's is "I'm Loving' It" has become popular with consumers worldwide. It has become a largest food service and supplier in the world because of its Product and service variety and quality. With the first outlet opening in Mumbai, it entered the India in the year 1996 by forming two 50:50 joint ventures, one with Hardcastle Restaurants Private Ltd. And other with Connaught Plaza Restaurants Private Ltd. In India.

The major task in hand for McDonalds faced in India of diversified culture. Majority of consumers in India were vegetarians, and some are non-vegetarians with distinct exclusion to beef and pork. Additionally, the price points were too high for the Indian consumers affordability. McDonald's was famed for its hamburgers which are made from beef and pork burgers. But due to religious reason consumers for satisfaction of their demand and preference it came up with the chicken and fish burgers. It has made separate kitchen in the outlet considering non vegetarian customers traditions. So, there was a lot of study has been done by the company on its product and service categories keeping in mind the habits and price suitability of consumers. There was a fierce competition from the lots of local food retailers who were quite experienced and had an edge over McDonald's in terms of knowledge of local tastes and price.

Most appealing task for McDonald was its marketing strategy flexibility. It was imperative for it to come up with localisation of its products for meeting the requirements and expectation of its consumers. Consumers were assured of no beef and pork menu and also there are a variety of option in the vegetarian menu. In Gujarat the restaurant serves on its menu product variations, keeping in mind the interest of the Jain population, which is particularly avoids eating any form of root vegetables. Then very recently it inaugurated world's first all vegetarian restaurant in every religious pilgrimage sites of India.

By means of strategic moves McDonald sensed Indian consumers are price sensitive so the Happy price menu was launched, which gave attention on the family fun elements as well. With localisation of the menu in terms of pricing as well, McDonalds came up with introducing varieties of burgers of 20 rupees called Aloo Tikki, a cutlet made of mashed potatoes, peas and flavoured with spices, McSpicy, and special range of Cheese. Today in India there are 350 outlets of McDonalds, and they foresee huge target consumers base, and also they plan to push it beyond 1000 outlets. Recently McDonald have a website where you can ask questions and then company will respond with various options as solutions. It's called our food, your question. It is the commitment of McDonald's to deliver high quality, safe and healthy food. It's food product recognizes the relationship between a balanced diet, lifestyle and health for consumer healthy living. The success of the social media strategy by McDonald's has enabled it map its strategies properly. The Golden Arches is said to be perfect and most recognizable symbol in the world. For its marketing and promotions and customer engagement McDonald's used social media. In Facebook McDonald's is more popular with more than 78.5 Million followers and 3.3 million followers on Instagram, 3.5 million followers on Twitter which has a large fan base for a fast food chain brand.

•••

Coca-Cola

Coca-Cola, is among the largest and oldest leading player in the Indian beverage market. In the year 1993, after liberalization of Indian market Coca Cola had lead the market by acquiring all its competitors soft drinks brands in the market like Thums-up, Limca, and Gold Spot by using its expertise.

Its operations include over 7,000 Indian distributors and more than 2.2 million retailers, have grown rapidly through a model that supports bottling operations, both companies owned as well as locally owned. Today, the brands are leading brands in most beverage segments. The Company's brands in India comprises of Coca-Cola, Fanta Orange, Limca, Sprite, Thumps Up, Burn, Kinley, Maaza, Minute Maid Pulpy Orange, Minute Maid Nimbu Fresh and the Georgia Gold range of teas and coffees and Vitingo.

Now Coca-cola is present in the market with product portfolio of a 60 percent share in the carbonated soft drinks under the name of Coca-cola, Thumbs up, Sprite, 36 percent share in fruit drinks labelled as Mazaa, Pulpy Orange and 33 per cent share in the packaged water segment, Kinley. During this period, the controversy related to pesticide tarnished the image of the company by bringing down the sales by 11 percent.

Initially Coca-Cola entered the Indian market during the late 1970s and the Government's subsequent order had forced the company to leave. The company again made an re-entry into the India in the year 1993, as with liberalization of market again. Working on the infrastructure the company spent a whooping US$ 1bn for succeeding in India. Then in India company has investment in setting-up 25 wholly owned bottling plants. All these steps taken by the company ensured that the company had a deeper level of penetration in the Indian market, even in the rural areas.

It went ahead with global communications only while re-launching the Coca-Cola brand in India, but sooner it realized its mistake and the company quickly adapted its local communication to ensure proper appeal for consumers in Indian market. The company rode on two of the strongest pillars, a brand can use in Indian advertisement and communication industry is of Bollywood and Cricket. It roped in a number of celebrity film stars and cricketers for promoting its brand in the Indian market. Its various promotional campaign with the tag line —Thanda matlab Coca-Cola was able to create the mass appeal.

For positioning the brand Coca-Cola for rural consumers, the company roped in Aamir Khan the famous Bollywood star. Company made the entry level price of its product to Rs.5, only to further deep root presence in rural market.

Successfully the company also overcame the biggest challenge it faced in the year 2003 of the pesticide controversy. As the company well along came up with airing an advertisement which provided a tour of the Coca-Cola factory and showcased how the 400 quality control tests are a part of the production process so as to revive the trust of the consumers. Now with all these social and cultural issues, customers are using Coca-Cola due to its strong brand reputation all over the world. The reason being that Indian youngsters are now consuming more soft drinks. Yet however, with many studies and policy changes, Coca-Cola will be able to establish its brand reputation and increase its market share in the near future. Also, they are eyeing India to be one of the top five global markets.

*****

References

1. P.C. Jain, Monica Bhatt, Consumer Behaviour (2ndEd.), New Delhi, S. Chand
2. Solomon, Consumer Behaviour- Buying, Having and Being (11thEd.), New Delhi, Pearson Education
3. Philip Kotler, Kevin Lane Keller, Abraham Koshy, Mithileshwar Jha, Marketing Management (13thEd.), New Delhi, Pearson Education
4. M. Govindarajan, Marketing Management (2ndEd.), New Delhi, Prentice Hall
5. Harsh V Verma, Brand Management (2ndEd.), New Delhi, Excel Book
6. www.wikipedia.org
7. www.ibef.org
8. www.businessjargons.com
9. www.business-standard.com
10. http://harishbhijoor.blogspot.com/
11. www.afaqs.com
12. https://www.kelloggs.in/
13. https://www.mcdonaldsindia.com/
14. https://www.coca-colaindia.com/
15. http://www.socialresearchfoundation.com/

www.ingramcontent.com/pod-product-compliance
Lightning Source LLC
Chambersburg PA
CBHW070817220526
45466CB00002B/687